Original title:
The Snooze Button Serenade

Copyright © 2024 Creative Arts Management OÜ
All rights reserved.

Author: Nathaniel Blackwood
ISBN HARDBACK: 978-9916-90-522-7
ISBN PAPERBACK: 978-9916-90-523-4

Ballad of Another Day Deferred

A morning missed, the sun now low,
Promises whispered, so hard to sow.
Chasing dreams that drift away,
In shadows cast by yesterday.

The clock ticks down, the moments fade,
With every choice, a price is paid.
Yet hope still lingers in the air,
For dreams deferred, we still can dare.

The Quiet Call of Comfortable Night

The stars alight, a gentle glow,
In whispers soft, the breezes flow.
Embrace the calm, release the day,
Let quiet thoughts just drift away.

The moonbeams dance upon your cheek,
In stillness found, the heart can speak.
Close your eyes, the world is wide,
In dreams, my dear, you shall abide.

Rhythm of the Reluctant Rise

The dawn peeks in, a soft refrain,
Reluctant hearts, yet pulls the chain.
With heavy eyelids, morning light,
We greet the day with muted sighs.

The blankets hold, the warmth is near,
To linger long, to shed the fear.
But life persists and bids us stand,
In rhythmic dance, we take our hand.

Daybreak's Faintest Whisper

A shimmer glows on distant shores,
The day awakes, but softly implores.
To listen close, to heed the sound,
As light unfolds on hallowed ground.

The whispers rise, both sweet and clear,
Inviting dreams that linger near.
In every breeze, a story told,
Of daybreak's grace, both soft and bold.

Morning Melodies of Reluctant Dreams

Softly breaking light spills in,
Awakens thoughts of yesterday's spin.
Birds are singing, hearts in flight,
Morning whispers gently, oh so slight.

Coffee brews, aroma's tease,
Waking up is never a breeze.
Clouds drift by, dreams start to fade,
In this dawn, new memories are made.

Sunlight dances on window panes,
Breaking through the night's dark chains.
Fleeting moments, softly gleaned,
In morning's arms, all is redeemed.

Promises linger in the air,
Hope and warmth, a gentle care.
With each note, life starts to hum,
In melodies, the day will come.

Chasing the Whisper of Sleep

Night's embrace still clings so tight,
Chasing dreams with fading light.
Soft shadows linger, hopes entwined,
Silhouettes of what we hoped to find.

Moonlight drapes the silent ground,
In darkness, only whispers found.
Memories beckon, softly speak,
In this chase, we dare to seek.

Stars above, a scattered sigh,
Chronicles of those who fly.
Weaving tales of hidden lore,
In our hearts, a distant shore.

Let the night pull us beneath,
Where dreams are born and linger sheath.
Chasing whispers, soft and deep,
In the silence, we will keep.

The Dance of Delayed Dawn

Colors blend, the sky so bright,
Brushstrokes of a new day's light.
Time stands still as shadows sway,
In the embrace of the breaking day.

Clouds pirouette, a gentle tease,
Fading stars, bending on the breeze.
Moments linger, hearts in tune,
The world awakens, not a moment too soon.

Chasing daylight, lost in the glow,
As the horizon starts to flow.
Nature's waltz, a tender call,
In this dance, we're part of it all.

Lost in rhythm, joy takes flight,
As dawn unfolds with pure delight.
With every step, we find our song,
In the dance where we belong.

Lullabies for the Late Riser

Whispers hush as soft winds blow,
Beneath blankets, dreams still grow.
Morning calls with gentle plea,
Awakening the soul, let it be free.

The clock ticks loud but heart beats slow,
Wrapped in warmth, holding on, let go.
Each melody a tender plea,
For moments sweet, simply to be.

Outside, life begins to hum,
While within, stillness has come.
Every heartbeat sings the refrain,
In lullabies that soothe the brain.

So take your time, dear heart of mine,
In late risings, beauty align.
Each breath a note in soft embrace,
In these lullabies, find your place.

Whispered Morning Threnody

In the dawn's soft light, shadows play,
Dreams linger lightly, drift away.
Whispers of night, secrets unveil,
Morning's embrace, a bittersweet tale.

Echoes of slumber, bid goodbye,
Underneath clouds, the sun will sigh.
Gentle hues burn, a canvas aglow,
Time unravels, as moments flow.

In the silence, hearts softly ache,
Yearning for dreams, awake, awake!
Yet the world calls, with urgent grace,
A tender farewell, to night's embrace.

Slumber's Sweet Protest

Nestled in blankets, a fortress so warm,
Against the day's chaos, a peaceful charm.
Eyes weary of light, plead for reprieve,
In the arms of slumber, I wish to believe.

The clock ticks loudly, a tyrant's decree,
Yet dreams softly whisper, just stay here with me.
Moments suspended, where time holds its breath,
In a world of allure, I flirt with sweet death.

Yet morning pulls firmly, with warmth and with light,
Stirring the senses, dispelling the night.
Still I resist, savoring the pause,
In slumber's sweet protest, a noble cause.

Chronicles of a Sleepyhead

Once upon a cozy night, dreams did weave,
A sleepyhead's tale, in slumber to believe.
Stars above winked, softly they sang,
While under the moon, sweet drowsiness sprang.

In realms of wonder, adventures untold,
Where shadows dance and laughter unfolds.
A tapestry spun from eyelids so light,
Chronicles flourish in the heart of the night.

With each gentle sigh, a new page turns,
In a sleepy embrace, the spirit yearns.
For every new dawn that breaks on the shore,
Marks the end of the tales, but opens the door.

Wakeful Dilemmas

Restless thoughts swirl, like leaves in the breeze,
Caught in a dance, unease never leaves.
The clock chimes softly, reminding me still,
Of dreams left behind, of hopes unfulfilled.

Awake in this world, where silence screams loud,
I ponder the paths, both humble and proud.
With choices like shadows, they flicker and fade,
And in the light's glare, my fears are displayed.

Yet dawn's gentle fingers, brush against my skin,
With whispers of courage, to rise up within.
So I wrestle and ponder, embrace what I may,
In the realm of the wakeful, I find my own way.

Dreamers' Dilemma at Dawn

In shadows soft, the dreams do play,
As night fades slowly into day.
Whispers linger, hopes entwined,
Yet sunlight beckons, truth unkind.

Wings of sleep, they flutter still,
Caught between the heart and will.
A world outside, it calls so clear,
But dreams hold tight, they linger near.

Choices clash, the mind a maze,
To linger long or greet the rays.
Heartbeats quicken, moments sway,
In dawn's embrace, we drift away.

Awake to find the silence break,
To choose a path, our lives to make.
The dreamers' plea, a sweet refrain,
At dawn's first light, we break the chain.

Ode to the Half-Woken Heart.

Awake but lost, the heart does drift,
Between the dreams and daylight's gift.
A tender ache, a muted song,
In morning's glow, we feel so wrong.

Softly yearning, the spirit sighs,
For night's embrace, for starry skies.
Yet here we stand, in soft sunrise,
A half-woken heart, with heavy eyes.

The world demands a voice to raise,
But all I feel is dreamy haze.
A battle waged with every beat,
To wake, to love, to feel complete.

In this twilight, I find my place,
Between the worlds, a tender space.
Ode to the heart, so full yet sore,
Whispers of dreams and so much more.

Morning's Lullaby

Softly sings the morning light,
Wrapping dreams in warmth so bright.
Birds begin their sweet ballet,
As night's embrace fades away.

Gentle breezes whisper low,
Through the leaves, their laughter flows.
Nature calls in vibrant tones,
Her lullaby, our hearts' own homes.

Colors bloom as shadows flee,
A canvas bright, for all to see.
Each moment cherished, every sigh,
In morning's arms, we learn to fly.

Let the day unfold its grace,
Wrapped in light, we find our place.
With every note, the journey starts,
Morning's lullaby fills our hearts.

Dreamy Delays

Time tiptoes on silken threads,
As thoughts drift lightly in our heads.
Moments linger, slipping slow,
Lost in reverie, we let them flow.

The clock keeps ticking, but we stay,
Caught in the web of dreams at play.
In cozy corners, visions twirl,
As sunrise murmurs, dreams unfurl.

A fleeting glance, a whispered wish,
The world outside, a tempting dish.
Yet here we nest, so warm, so fine,
In dreamy delays, we sip our time.

Awake, perhaps, but so half-lost,
To leave this place would come at cost.
In the haze of morning's light,
We hold our dreams, just out of sight.

Lullabies of Limitless Time

Whispers of dreams dance in the night,
Stars glimmer softly, embracing the light.
Every heartbeat slows, a gentle refrain,
Cradled in shadows, we feel no pain.

Time drifts like clouds in a twilight sky,
Moments unfold, as the world whispers by.
Each sigh a promise, each lull a prayer,
In this vast silence, we find our care.

Morning's Sassy Sigh

Sunlight tumbles through the window wide,
Casting playful shadows, where dreams reside.
A coffee cup brims with warmth and cheer,
Morning's laughter is all that we hear.

Birds sing a tune, so daringly bold,
Breaking the stillness with stories retold.
Each ray of light teases the night away,
Inviting the world to dance and play.

Twilight's Tender Lament

The sky bleeds colors of crimson and gold,
A whispering breeze, stories unfold.
Shadows stretch long, as the day bids goodbye,
Holding the secrets of stars in the sky.

Each moment a memory, bittersweet grace,
Twilight caresses the earth's gentle face.
Sighs of the evening blend soft with the night,
Embracing the darkness, holding on tight.

The Rhapsody of Repose

In quiet corners, peace softly dwells,
Where silence unfolds its tender spells.
The weight of the day gently slips away,
As dreams weave their magic at the end of day.

Soft pillows cradle, like clouds in the air,
A haven of comfort, a treasured care.
Each heartbeat finds rhythm in moments so slow,
In the rhapsody of repose, let love overflow.

Slumber's Sweetest Refrain

In the quiet night, dreams softly glide,
Whispers of comfort, where shadows reside.
Moonbeams like silk, drape over the floor,
Cradling the weary, inviting for more.

Gentle the silence, wrapped in its charm,
Every heartbeat sighs, finding the harm.
Lullabies linger, as stars start to wink,
Flowing like water, in night's soothing drink.

Clouds softly dance, like thoughts in a daze,
Time ticks away, lost in the haze.
Nestled in twilight, where worries subside,
Slumber's sweet music, a comforting guide.

Awake to the dawn, but hold onto dreams,
Morning light stretches, its golden beams.
Yet in sleep's embrace, we find our own grace,
Slumber's sweetest refrain, our quietest place.

The Art of Postponing Daylight

When dawn breaks gently, I close my eyes tight,
In warmth of my bed, I resist the first light.
The world waits outside, with a call I can feel,
Yet here in this moment, my heart makes a deal.

Shadows are casting, the room holds me close,
Each tick of the clock feels like a solemn dose.
Wrapped in the calm, I breathe in the night,
The art of postponing, a delicate fight.

Time flows like a river, each minute a dream,
Fleeting as wisps of a soft, silver gleam.
The morning can wait, I'm lost in this trance,
The sun can hold off, while I take a chance.

So let the day linger, let moments align,
With silence my canvas, and peace is the sign.
In the art of postponing, the daylight can pause,
For here in the stillness, I find my own cause.

Hushed Anthems of the Drowsy

Silent serenades, the night softly hums,
Each note a cocoon, where weariness comes.
Under the covers, I drift in a sway,
Hushed anthems of drowsy, at end of the day.

The stars whisper secrets, the moon shares a tune,
Rocking the dreamers, beneath the pale moon.
Echoes of twilight, a calm lullaby,
Wrap me in shadows, as time flutters by.

Each sigh becomes music, each breath finds a beat,
The world slips away, as I rest my feet.
Hushed antiphons cradle, the weight of my sleep,
Where memories linger, in the stillness they seep.

So let me succumb, to this sweet serenade,
In arms of the night, my worries will fade.
Hushed anthems of drowsy, a cherished refrain,
In slumber's embrace, I'll surely remain.

Rhapsody in Five More Minutes

Just five more minutes, let time hold its breath,
Wrapped in the stillness, I banish all debts.
A world full of tasks, can wait just a while,
In dreams I will wander, with peace as my style.

The alarm clock's a thief, steals dreams from my mind,
Yet here in this moment, my worries unwind.
Clouds drift through my thoughts, painting colors so
bright,
A rhapsody whispers, as I clutch the night.

With pillows as clouds, I soar and I glide,
Through realms full of laughter, nowhere to hide.
Each tick of the clock becomes music so sweet,
In rhapsody's grasp, I find my heartbeat.

Five more minutes, the world can wait slow,
In silken embrace, where gentle winds blow.
Let me stay dreaming, with stars shining clear,
A rhapsody cherished, this moment I hold dear.

Lament of the Morning Moon

In silence she weeps, the morning light,
Her silver glow dims, fading from sight.
A dream that once danced in the night air,
Now lost to the sun, stripped bare and rare.

She whispers to stars, a soft goodbye,
While shadows retreat, beneath the sky.
Beneath the blue wake, she softly glows,
Her sorrow fulfilled in the dawn's close.

Silent vows made in twilight's grace,
Yet warm are the tears on her pale face.
In the hush of dawn, she takes her flight,
The essence of night, dissipating light.

But when day departs, she'll rise anew,
Reclaimed by the dark, the vast and true.
Her beauty will linger, a hushed refrain,
In shadows of twilight, she'll shine again.

A Haiku for Hibernation

Winter's breath whispers,
Soft blankets of white embrace,
Dreams sleep, still and deep.

Chill winds cradle trees,
Nature's pause in breaths of snow,
Time lingers in peace.

Stars blink in the frost,
Quiet echoes of heartbeats,
The world holds its sigh.

Underneath the gloom,
Life waits for warmth to return,
A promise of bloom.

Suspended Moments

In a fleeting space, time holds its breath,
Each heartbeat a whisper, a dance with death.
Framed in stillness, dreams take flight,
Moments linger, painted in light.

The clock ticks slowly, shadows entwined,
In the grasp of the now, the past is blind.
Glimpses of laughter, echoes of sighs,
Caught in the web of our shared goodbyes.

Footsteps soft echo in morning's glaze,
Casting reflections through foggy haze.
Suspended in wonder, we seize the cause,
Finding forever in brief applause.

As dusk draws near, the world stands still,
Chasing the twilight, a quiet thrill.
In this sacred silence, hearts collide,
Moments eternal, no need to hide.

The Comfort of Darkness

In shadows we find solace, sweet embrace,
A gentle caress, a secret place.
Where worries dissolve, and dreams can soar,
Wrapped in the night, we crave for more.

The stars are our witnesses, bright and true,
Guiding the way through shades of blue.
We dance on the edge of dreams unspun,
Our souls come alive, lost but not done.

Whispers of night sing tender songs,
Unraveling time with their silken throngs.
In darkness, we gather, together as one,
Finding our strength 'til the morning has spun.

So let us hold close the depth of the night,
For in every shadow, there glimmers a light.
Embrace all the whispers, the calm, and the fear,
In the comfort of darkness, we draw ever near.

A Serenade for the WEary

In twilight's arms, the weary sigh,
Beneath the stars that softly cry.
Whispers weave through silent nights,
As dreams take wing on feathered flights.

Worn shoes rest, the journey done,
While moonlit serenades are spun.
Hearts unlace from daily grind,
In this sweet hush, solace we find.

Each note a balm for weary souls,
Creating peace, the heart extols.
In shadows long, past burdens fade,
As night's warm cloak begins to braid.

A melody drifts on gentle air,
Healing, soothing every care.
Let the world spin far away,
In serenade, the weary stay.

Notes from a Dreamy Battleground

In fields of gold where shadows dance,
Our dreams collide, we take the chance.
With every heartbeat, we engage,
Across the night, we find the page.

The echoes of our memories fade,
In sleepy fog, the mind parade.
Stars twinkle like a distant fire,
As dreams unravel, daring, higher.

In battles fought with softest dreams,
Awake we ponder silent themes.
Yet here we stand, both brave and mild,
In this dual realm, forever wild.

Let whispers guide as we explore,
The hidden truths we can't ignore.
In nightly realms, we boldly roam,
Creating worlds we call our own.

The Tranquil Tease of Slumber

The hush of night begins to swell,
In hidden depths where secrets dwell.
A gentle pull, a soft embrace,
In slumber's arms, we find our place.

With every breath, the world recedes,
In tranquil dreams, the spirit feeds.
Whispers float on sighs of night,
Inviting thoughts to take their flight.

Soft pillows cradle minds adrift,
In this stillness, we receive the gift.
Time slows down, the heart beats slow,
As shadows weave with moonlit glow.

In tranquil tease, we drift and sway,
Let go of fears that haunt the day.
With open hearts and quiet glee,
We dive into eternity.

Cadence of the Can't-get-up

The morning light spills through the shade,
Yet here I lie, in dreams delayed.
A dance of sheets, my cozy trap,
In gentle folds, I take a nap.

With coffee calling from afar,
I close my eyes and hear the spar.
The world outside begins to hum,
But in my dreams, I'm feeling numb.

With each soft chime, the clocks betray,
The rhythm of a lazy day.
In this embrace, I wish to stay,
Where worries fade and hopes can play.

The cadence sings, so sweet and low,
As drifting thoughts like rivers flow.
In stillness found, I lay my claim,
This sacred pause, my heart's refrain.

Waking in Slow Motion

In the morning's gentle sway,
Dreams linger, softly stay.
Sunlight drips like honey sweet,
Time moves slow, in soft retreat.

Eyes peel open, mind a haze,
Moments stretch in hazy daze.
The world, a canvas unconfined,
Brushstrokes linger in the mind.

Whispers of the night unwind,
Floating thoughts, the heart aligned.
Each heartbeat takes a breath, a chance,
In this slow, melodic dance.

With every dawn, a new embrace,
In the quiet, find your place.
Waking slow, the world unfolds,
A story whispered, softly told.

Refrain of the Restful

In the stillness, peace reclaims,
Softly singing, gentle aims.
Breath by breath, with each repose,
The heart finds where the stillness goes.

Moments linger, sweet and serene,
In the hush, life's pulse is seen.
Nature's sigh, a soothing balm,
Here in quiet, all is calm.

Within the folds of tranquil time,
Restful thoughts begin to chime.
A symphony of silence plays,
In this haven, peace conveys.

Embrace the quiet, let it flow,
In restful arms, the spirit glows.
With each whisper, find your tune,
In the stillness, morning's bloom.

Pantomime of the Pillow

Soft as clouds, a silent stage,
Where dreams dance free, uncaged.
The pillow partners in the night,
Cradling thoughts till morning light.

In the shadows, whispers play,
Making stories fade away.
An echo of a lover's sigh,
In cozy confines, spirits fly.

Every crease and every fold,
Bears the secrets that it holds.
A pantomime in quiet grace,
Where heartstrings find their resting place.

As dawn arrives, the roles transform,
In daylight's glow, new dreams are born.
The pillow, keeper of the night,
Holds memories 'til the light.

The Lure of Lovelorn Sheets

Cocooned within their warm embrace,
The sheets hold love in every trace.
A tapestry of soft caress,
In tangled comfort, hearts confess.

Every wrinkle tells a tale,
Of dreams that danced, of love unveiled.
In twilight's glow, they gently sigh,
Cradling hopes that never die.

Subtle shadows play on white,
In the stillness, hearts ignite.
The sheets, a bridge from night to day,
Where whispered thoughts can drift away.

Thus, the lure of lovelorn sheets,
In quiet corners, heartbeats meet.
Under their watch, the world feels right,
In the gentle pull of love's delight.

The Lure of However Much Longer

The clock ticks slow, yet dreams collide,
In whispered hopes where hearts reside.
Time stretches thin, yet feels so bright,
With every glance, we chase the light.

Yet here we stand, caught in the sway,
Of fleeting moments, day by day.
The lure of 'how much longer' grows,
As time unfurls, the tension shows.

With every wish, we seek the dawn,
In shadows cast, the fears are drawn.
But through the dance of dusk and glare,
We find the strength to breathe, to care.

So let us hold this fleeting hour,
With all the grace of blooming flower.
For in the end, it's love we glean,
Through every struggle, every dream.

Compositions of Comfort and Coziness

In soft-lit rooms where shadows play,
Warm blankets wrap the chill away.
A cup of tea, steam rising high,
With gentle whispers, the world slips by.

Coziness finds us in a nook,
Lost in pages of a cherished book.
The laughter shared, the stories spun,
In those small moments, life is won.

Fires crackle, the night unfolds,
With every ember, a warmth to hold.
Beside the hearth, together we lean,
In compositions of light, serene.

Embrace the stillness, breathe it in,
Where love resides, and joys begin.
In cozy corners, we find our place,
Wrapped in comfort, a soft embrace.

The Plea for Peaceful Minutes

In hectic days that rush past me,
I seek the still, the calm, the free.
A moment's hush, a gentle sigh,
To pause, to breathe, to simply try.

Each ticking second draws me near,
To quiet paths where thoughts are clear.
The world can wait; it's time for me,
To savor silence endlessly.

For in this plea, my heart finds grace,
In slower steps, I find my place.
Where peace exists, no noise to break,
In tranquil minutes, I awake.

So heed my call for gentle hours,
To bloom in stillness like sweet flowers.
In peaceful minutes, life is spun,
A world of calm, in which we run.

Reveries Wrapped in Sheets

In daytime dreams, we softly drift,
With thoughts like clouds, they gently lift.
Wrapped in sheets, the world feels far,
In sleepy whispers, we're who we are.

Comfort calls within this space,
With shadows dancing, we find grace.
Swayed by visions, hearts take flight,
Through woven dreams of day and night.

The sun peeks in, a golden ray,
Yet here within, we long to stay.
In reverie's hold, the hours spin,
With quiet thoughts, we draw within.

So let us linger, soft and light,
In cozy corners, holding tight.
For dreams are woven in the sheets,
Our hearts united, where love beats.

Silence of the Sleeping Anew

In shadows soft, the silence lies,
As dreams weave tales beneath closed eyes.
The world outside fades to a hush,
In this cocoon, there's no need to rush.

Whispers of night cradle weary hearts,
In this stillness, a new day starts.
The rustling leaves sing a gentle tune,
Beneath the watchful, silver moon.

Each breath a lull, a calming wave,
In twilight's hold, the soul is brave.
With every pause, in peace we dwell,
In silence, we find our magic spell.

Awake, the dawn sweetly calls,
From slumber's grip, the spirit sprawls.
Yet in this quiet, warmth remains,
In sleeping's embrace, joy sustains.

Ephemeral Embrace

A fleeting touch upon my skin,
In twilight's glow, the day wears thin.
Moments dance like fireflies bright,
In the fragile hush of the encroaching night.

The world around begins to fade,
In this embrace, my fears are laid.
Your laughter ripples through the air,
An echo sweet, beyond compare.

But time, it flows like shifting sand,
Each heartbeat draws us close, yet spanned.
In the briefest warmth, love spins its thread,
Through stolen glances, softly said.

We remain lost in this fleeting glee,
A moment shared, just you and me.
To hold it tight, we dare to dream,
In the ephemeral, we find our theme.

The Dance of Drowsiness

In the quiet room, the shadows sway,
As heaviness drifts, fading the day.
A gentle lull, a whispered sigh,
In the dance of drowsiness, we lie.

The heart beats slow, as time drips down,
In soft repose, we cast the crown.
Sleep's tender fingers weave in and out,
In this sweet space, we dream without doubt.

The air grows thick with unspoken peace,
As thoughts entwine, and chaos cease.
A waltz of sighs, a ballet of grace,
In dreams, we find a timeless place.

Let the world turn, outside our door,
In this silent rhythm, we crave for more.
Together we drift, in night's embrace,
A dance of drowsiness, we trace.

A Slow Sunrise Anthem

Beneath the veil of the waking dawn,
The world unfurls, the night withdrawn.
A canvas stretches, kissed by light,
As colors blend, reclaiming sight.

With whispers soft, the sun ascends,
Bringing warmth, where shadows end.
Each ray a note in nature's song,
As melodies rise, sweet and strong.

The day awakes, a gentle sigh,
In the rhythm of life, we find our why.
As birds take flight, they serenade,
A slow sunrise, a grand parade.

Embrace the glow, let your spirit soar,
In this anthem of light, be evermore.
Each moment dawns, a chance to find,
The beauty within, the heart aligned.

The Velvet of Undisturbed Hours

In the stillness of the night,
every whisper softly glows.
The moon drapes a silver shroud,
as time gently ebbs and flows.

Thoughts drift like autumn leaves,
in a dreamscape only few know.
Each moment feels suspended,
in the velvet of the slow.

Stars twinkle like distant hopes,
telling tales of what's to come.
In the quiet, hearts can speak,
in a language soft and numb.

Embraced by shadows' grace,
we celebrate the peace of now.
In these hours, we find solace,
in the pages we allow.

Resisting the Call of Day

The dawn creeps with soft insistence,
its fingers brush the sleepy vale.
Yet here in twilight's tender arms,
I savor every dream and tale.

The night, a cloak of endless charm,
wraps me in its hushed refrain.
Each star, a pulse of distant light,
keeps me from the morning's strain.

Whispers linger in the shadows,
a gentle promise in the hue.
I breathe in the calm of starlight,
resisting what I thought I knew.

Let the sun ascend to blaze,
I dwell in night's sweet embrace.
For here, I'll linger in my dreams,
unfettered by the day's swift race.

Enchanted by Night's Embrace

Underneath the velvet sky,
where silence wraps the world in peace.
Night's embrace, a soothing balm,
invites the mind to find release.

Moonlight waltzes on the sea,
with gentle waves that kiss the shore.
In shadows deep, I lose my way,
searching for what I can't ignore.

A symphony of rustling leaves,
carries secrets in the breeze.
I'm enchanted by the stillness,
where every heartbeat feels at ease.

With every star, a wish reborn,
in the silence, I find my place.
For in the night, I am alive,
wrapped in twilight's warm embrace.

A Lullaby of Late Comings

In the quiet hour of dusk,
shadows dance on whispered dreams.
The night sings a gentle tune,
as the world softly redeems.

Stars peek through the tapestry,
telling stories, old and new.
With a sigh, I welcome them,
knowing well their secret view.

Time slips in a tender drift,
where worries fade and hopes renew.
A lullaby wrapped in silver,
beckoning me to rest, pursue.

Though late comings may feel lost,
they're merely paths yet to unfold.
In the depths of night, I find,
all the treasures yet untold.

The Beauty of Being Late

Life's a dance, don't rush the step,
Moments linger, secrets kept.
In the quiet, time expands,
Chasing dreams with open hands.

Colors bloom in twilight's glow,
Paths unfold, there's space to grow.
Every pause, a chance to breathe,
In the stillness, we believe.

Echoes from Dream Land

In the silence where shadows play,
Dreams weave whispers, soft as clay.
Stars align in velvet skies,
Reality blurs where wonder lies.

Flickering lights in distant streams,
Carrying hope on paper wings.
Every heartbeat, a tale untold,
In this realm, we're brave and bold.

Ode to Indecision

On the edge of paths unknown,
Choices linger, seeds are sown.
The heart wavers, thoughts entwine,
In the silence, we define.

What ifs dance in hazy light,
Torn between the day and night.
Each option beckons, whisper low,
In the crossroads, I must grow.

Surrendered to Slumber

In the night where dreams are spun,
Lullabies dance, day is done.
Clouds embrace the silent street,
Rest will wrap me, soft and sweet.

Fading echoes of the day,
In the dark, I drift away.
With the stars as guides above,
I surrender, wrapped in love.

Crescendo of the Cozy Cocoon

Wrapped in warmth, a soft embrace,
A world outside, a distant place.
Gentle whispers fill the air,
Nestled deep, without a care.

The blanket folds like wings in flight,
Cradling dreams that dance at night.
In this haven, solace found,
Where time stands still, and hearts unbound.

Crackling fires lend golden glow,
As shadows waltz, moving slow.
In twilight's hum, sweet comfort sings,
An orchestra of simple things.

With every sigh, the worries fade,
In this cocoon, life's charade.
The crescendo builds—a perfect sound,
In restful peace, true joy is found.

The Prelude to Awakening

Morning light begins to creep,
Through the curtains, secrets seep.
Whispers of the day ahead,
In the solace of soft bed.

A gentle stretch, a yawn so wide,
Warmth of dreams begins to slide.
Birdsong sings, a tune so bright,
Calling forth the dawn's delight.

Each second counts, the world awaits,
As slumber drapes and hesitates.
In this moment, peace resides,
A tranquil heart where hope abides.

Soon to rise, yet still we stay,
In this prelude to the day.
The tapestry of life will weave,
But here, dear rest, we still believe.

Symphony of the Sleepy Eyes

In the stillness, eyelids fall,
Soft and heavy, gently call.
The world a blur, a soothing haze,
Wrapped in twilight, lost in daze.

Melodies of dreams take flight,
In hushed tones, the stars are bright.
Each note a kiss upon the skin,
Lulling thoughts from deep within.

Whispers float on gentle breeze,
Carrying secrets, tales to tease.
In the symphony of night we find,
A harmony of heart and mind.

As sleep envelops, shadows play,
Guiding souls till break of day.
In sleepy eyes, such wisdom lies,
A serenade beneath the skies.

Echoes of Wishes for Rest

In the quiet, wishes bloom,
Softly filling every room.
Echoes dance on moonlit trails,
Carrying dreams on gentle sails.

Each heart whispers, seeking peace,
Longing for a sweet release.
With every breath, a prayer is sent,
A hope for solace, time well spent.

Stars above begin to shine,
Reminders that the night is divine.
In restful pause, all burdens cease,
Embraced by shadows, finding ease.

So let the echoes softly sway,
As wishes guide us on our way.
In the embrace of calm and rest,
We gather dreams that feel the best.

Unfinished Dreams

In twilight's glow, they softly weave,
The tales of hopes that we believe.
Each flicker dims, yet still it gleams,
A canvas stretched with unfinished dreams.

Beneath the stars, they drift away,
Whispers lost in yesterday.
A heartbeat's sigh, a silent scream,
Awake again to those lost dreams.

Through shadows cast and echoes bright,
We search for paths in the fading light.
Yet in the night, our spirits beam,
Forever chasing unfinished dreams.

In every heart, they take their flight,
The hopes we hold, the fears we fight.
With every dawn, they softly scheme,
Carving more of our unfinished dreams.

The Interlude of Indulgence

In sweet excess, we find our bliss,
A whispered vow, a stolen kiss.
Moments linger, we take our chance,
In the interlude, we dare to dance.

With every sip, the world retreats,
In golden light, life tastes so sweet.
We breathe the warmth, escape the fray,
Lost in the moment, come what may.

Underneath the starry skies,
We find our truth in sweet disguise.
Life's fleeting joy, a tender trance,
In the interlude, we twirl and prance.

But time, the thief, will call us back,
To roads once lost, the fading track.
Yet in our hearts, the memories dance,
Forever held in that sweet romance.

Portrait of a Dreamer

A brush in hand, with gentle grace,
He paints a world, a timeless space.
With every stroke, his visions gleam,
Creating life as a lucid dream.

His heart a palette, rich and deep,
With dreams that stir and never sleep.
In colors bold, they twist and weave,
A portrait made, in hopes we believe.

Through whispered tales, the shadows play,
He captures time in bright array.
With eyes that see beyond the seam,
He shares the heart of every dreamer.

In canvas wide, his spirit flies,
Among the stars, the endless skies.
In every hue, a distant beam,
The world unfolds for every dreamer.

Chronicles of the Weary

In winding paths, the weary tread,
With burdens borne and dreams unsaid.
Through fields of doubt, they search for light,
In chronicles of the endless fight.

Each sigh a tale, each step a song,
In shadows deep, where the lost belong.
With weary hearts, they seek and strive,
To build a world where hopes revive.

Among the throngs, their spirits blend,
In silence shared, they find a friend.
Together bound, the journeys gleam,
In chronicles of a shared dream.

And with each dawn, their spirits stir,
Through fractures healed, the visions blur.
In every heart, a flicker gleams,
The chronicles of the hopeful dreams.

The Art of Hesitation

In shadows cast by doubt's soft glow,
We linger here, where answers flow.
A breath held tight, a whispered plea,
To choose a path, or set it free.

Moments stretch like elastic time,
With every thought, we start to climb.
Yet every peak hides silent fear,
We pause, reflect, then draw it near.

Around us swirls a gentle breeze,
The heartbeats quicken, thoughts unease.
In stillness lies the truth we seek,
A quiet dance, unspoken, meek.

Embrace the pause, the fragile wait,
In hesitation, we create.
A tapestry of dreams unfurled,
The art of life, in moments swirled.

Dawn's Gentle Resistance

The dawn breaks soft, with colors pale,
Whispers of night begin to sail.
Yet in this light, a shiver stands,
Resisting change like shifting sands.

Birds warble sweet, a tender call,
But shadows linger, weaving thrall.
Each ray of gold that starts to creep,
Awakens dreams we wish to keep.

The sky blushes, hesitant hue,
Reflecting all we thought we knew.
In vibrant dawn, we share our plight,
Embracing change with fading night.

With gentle hands, the sun ascends,
While night reluctantly still bends.
Eeach moment clings, a sweet embrace,
Dawn's resistance finds its place.

Twilight's Allure

The twilight falls, a velvet sigh,
As stars awake in dusky sky.
A hush descends on earth and stream,
Wrapped in the arms of night's soft dream.

The colors fade, a painter's brush,
In quiet calm, our worries hush.
Each moment lingers, sweet and still,
A time to ponder, reflect, and thrill.

Beneath the moon, our secrets hide,
In twilight's glow, we can confide.
The world transforms, a gentle guise,
As magic dances in our eyes.

Here in this hour, we find our peace,
In twilight's arms, our heartbeats cease.
A moment caught, without a care,
In twilight's allure, we breathe the air.

The Serenade of Sleepy Souls

The moonlight spills, a soft caress,
Embracing all in night's redress.
Whispers drift on gentle breeze,
A serenade that puts hearts at ease.

Sleepy souls in twilight dwell,
Cocooned in dreams, they softly swell.
With every heartbeat, night unfolds,
A tale of wonder waiting to be told.

Stars blink softly, a knowing dance,
Each twinkle holds a cherished chance.
To lose ourselves in boundless skies,
As sleep's warm tide gently flies.

In slumber's hug, the world recedes,
As starry night fulfills our needs.
The serenade of sleepy dreams,
Cradled in night's enchanted themes.

The Glistening Guilt of Another Snooze

The alarm rings sharp, a clear demand,
Yet sleep's embrace holds me, soft and bland.
Another five, just one more round,
In this cocoon where comfort is found.

The clock ticks on, my heart beats slow,
Guilt dances lightly in morning's glow.
Promises whispered, dreams left to fade,
As daylight stretches, and I've betrayed.

The world outside begins to race,
While I cocoon in this sleepy space.
The sun climbs high, a hopeful beam,
Yet here I linger, lost in a dream.

With every snooze, I weigh my choice,
A battle silent, without a voice.
Between the sheets, the guilt will cling,
As whispers of regret softly sing.

Harmonies Beneath the Covers

Soft whispers play under the quilt,
Melodies spun from dreams we've built.
Each breath a note, in this serene night,
Together we hum till morning light.

The world outside is far away,
In this cocoon where we wish to stay.
Fingers entwined, we share a tune,
Under the spell of the midnight moon.

Rhythms of warmth in shadows cast,
Memories linger, echoes of the past.
Every heartbeat, a steadfast chord,
In harmony sweet, our spirits soared.

As dawn approaches, our song will wane,
Yet in the daylight, love will remain.
For the best harmonies are never lost,
Beneath the covers, sharing the cost.

When Time Stands Still at Sunrise

Golden rays break the night's soft hold,
Each moment peaceful, vivid and bold.
Birds whisper secrets in the morning air,
As time suspends in this tranquil affair.

The world awakens, yet nothing stirs,
In this dawn, the magic occurs.
Colors blend in harmonious play,
Painting the sky a tender array.

Crisp air envelops, refreshing and bright,
Each breath a treasure, pure delight.
A pause in chaos, a gentle reprieve,
In the hush of sunrise, we truly believe.

Moments linger, as shadows recede,
In nature's embrace, we find what we need.
When time stands still, our hearts align,
In the beauty of dawn, everything's fine.

The Gentle Tug of Tempting Dreams

Lulled by whispers of nighttime's grace,
Dreams beckon softly, urging a trace.
In twilight's grasp, desires take flight,
A gentle tug into the night.

Visions adorn the edges of sleep,
Each thought a promise, the heart to keep.
With every flutter, a story unfolds,
In this realm where the brave and bold.

Floating on clouds made of sweet delight,
We chase shimmering stars, shining bright.
The moon's soft glow holds our secrets tight,
As gently we sway through the velvety night.

Yet dawn will come, and dreams must part,
But their echoes linger deep in the heart.
The gentle tug lingers in the mind,
As we wake to the world, so unkind.

Hibernation Hymn

In the quiet of the night,
Dreams take flight, out of sight.
Wrapped in warmth, the world sleeps,
As winter's hush softly creeps.

Stars glimmering like distant shores,
Nature whispers, softly roars.
Beneath the frost, life lingers still,
In peaceful rest, a tranquil thrill.

Close your eyes, let shadows play,
Rest from the toil of the day.
Time slows down, a gentle pause,
In hibernation, nature draws.

When spring awakens, life will bloom,
Casting away the silent gloom.
In slumber deep, new hopes unify,
A hymn of life beneath the sky.

Procrastination's Embrace

Time slips by like grains of sand,
Tasks await, yet I just stand.
In the comfort of delay,
Tomorrow holds what I won't say.

Dreams are swirling, just out of reach,
Promises made, but none to teach.
Goals fade softly into night,
Lost in whispers, out of sight.

The clock ticks on, a steady drum,
Yet here I sit, my mind goes numb.
Thoughts of action drift away,
As I find comfort in dismay.

But in the stillness, plans ignite,
A spark emerges, burning bright.
In procrastination's sweet embrace,
I'll find a way, I'll pick up pace.

The Prelude to Awakening

Morning whispers, soft and clear,
Sunlight stretches, drawing near.
A gentle yawn, the day unfolds,
With secret stories yet untold.

Birds are chirping, songs arise,
Painting colors in the skies.
As darkness fades, the world awakes,
Each moment fresh, as silence breaks.

Buds are blooming, life appears,
Wiping away the night's deep fears.
With every breath, the heart beats strong,
A prelude sweet to life's great song.

Embrace the dawn with open hands,
Step into light, where life expands.
Awakening the dreams we chase,
In every dawn, we find our place.

Melodies of Muffled Minutes

Time flows softly, a gentle stream,
Whispers echo, lost in dream.
Each second wrapped in velvet light,
Muffled minutes guard the night.

Underneath the moon's soft glow,
Silence weaves a tale, slow.
Each heartbeat sings a quiet tune,
Softly swaying 'neath the moon.

Moving shadows dance around,
In this stillness, peace is found.
Melodies linger, sweet and low,
In a world where wishes flow.

Let each moment, deeply felt,
Paint the stories life has dealt.
Find the music hidden deep,
In muffled minutes, secrets keep.

The Sleepy Siren Call

In the twilight, shadows grow,
Whispers soft in the dimming glow.
The siren sings, a dulcet tune,
Lulling dreams beneath the moon.

Candles flicker, dancing light,
Fading echoes of day turn night.
A gentle pull, the heart complies,
To journey where the slumber lies.

The tides do shift in tranquil seas,
As whispers ride on evening breeze.
A lullaby of night unfolds,
In dreams, a thousand tales retold.

With every note, the world retreats,
Embracing sleep, the heart then beats.
For in this call, we find our rest,
The sleepy siren, nature's best.

Bedtime's Battle Cry

The stars emerge, the war begins,
A battle fought where daylight ends.
In cozy forts, the children hide,
As dreams and fears collide inside.

The clock strikes eight, a thunder roars,
Pajamas worn like brave armors.
With pillows raised as shields so high,
Ready to face the night's sly lie.

Monsters loom in shadow's wake,
But bedtime's tales, like magic, break.
The courage found in whispered lore,
Turns fright to smiles forevermore.

At last, their eyes begin to close,
The battle won, as silence flows.
In dreams, adventures await anew,
Bedtime's cry, a soft adieu.

Song of the Waking World

In dawn's embrace, the light awakes,
The sleepy earth, a gentle shake.
Birdsong calls through fragrant air,
Each note a balm, beyond compare.

Golden rays on petals gleam,
Nature's brush, a waking dream.
The streams do gurgle, laughter bright,
As day unveils the velvet night.

Every leaf a story tells,
Of whispered winds and distant bells.
In meadows wide, where children play,
The song of life begins the day.

With every heartbeat, joy unfurls,
In this bright symphony of worlds.
Together, we rise, hand in hand,
To greet the dawn across the land.

Wistful Whispers of Wakefulness

A gentle sigh, the night is late,
In quiet corners, dreams await.
With every sound, a heart does sway,
Longing for the break of day.

The moon looks down with tender grace,
As shadows stretch in soft embrace.
What memories in silence creep,
In wistful whispers, close to sleep.

The stars disperse like scattered seeds,
Each one a wish on night's cool breeze.
In the stillness, thoughts take flight,
A tapestry of dark and light.

But morning comes with golden eyes,
To sweep away the starry skies.
Awake, we rise, from dreams unspun,
To greet the world, a new day begun.

Echoes of a Dreamer

In the still of night, whispers flow,
Thoughts entwined in a gentle glow.
Stars above whisper ancient lore,
While dreams awaken, longing for more.

Footsteps trace paths in the sands of time,
Chasing shadows, simple and sublime.
A heart that beats with the pulse of hope,
Navigates realms where the spirits cope.

In valleys of light, visions dance free,
Painting the night with a tapestry.
The echo of laughter, soft as a breeze,
Guiding the dreamer with effortless ease.

Awake, yet lost in a world of grace,
With every heartbeat, a cherished trace.
In the silence, the heart finds its tune,
While the moon smiles softly, a watchful boon.

A Symphony of Slumber

In quiet corners, shadows reside,
Melodies linger where secrets hide.
Each note whispers dreams, soft and sweet,
Cradling the weary in rhythmic retreat.

The lull of whispers, gentle and low,
Encircles the mind like falling snow.
Time waltzes lightly with stars up above,
While hearts settle down in the arms of love.

Clouds gather round, a comforting shroud,
Wrapping the world in a silken cloud.
As the symphony swells, soft and deep,
Morning waits patiently, tangled in sleep.

Awakening hearts with the first light of dawn,
The symphony fades, yet lingers on.
In dreams, we find pieces of ourselves,
Stories that rest on the quietest shelves.

Requiem for the Alarm

When the morning breaks, alarms sing loud,
Awakening souls from a shrouded cloud.
A requiem played for the night so still,
Where dreams entwined with the moon's sweet will.

Eyes flutter open to a harsh embrace,
The soft warmth of dreams begins to erase.
With one final chime, the past must retreat,
As reality calls with a rapid heartbeat.

Soft echoes linger of moments once shared,
In the sacred silence, the heart had dared.
Yet the dawn casts shadows that softly impinge,
On the fleeting visions that once did sing.

So here in the light, we find our way,
While the requiem fades with the softest gray.
Yet deep in our minds, the melodies stay,
A reminder of dreams that will never sway.

The Temptation of Pillow Clouds

Pillow clouds beckon with tender grace,
Whispers of slumber in a soft embrace.
Each sigh invites a journey anew,
Through realms where the wildest dreams come true.

Restless hearts yearn for the peace they crave,
In twilight's arms, they're destined to wave.
A dance of thoughts, light as a breeze,
Melting the worries, putting minds at ease.

In the cocoon of softness, we drift away,
Into the hush where the shadows play.
The temptation of rest sings sweet to the soul,
Whispering secrets that promise to console.

As dreams take flight on the wings of night,
Pillow clouds cradle with soft, gentle light.
And here in our hearts, we find our reprieve,
In the sanctuary where we dare to believe.

The Reluctant Rise

The dawn creeps in, a gentle light,
I pull the sheets, my silent fight.
Dreams linger soft, like whispered air,
Yet morning calls, it's time to dare.

With heavy eyes, I face the day,
Yet in my heart, the dreams still play.
A weary soul in morning's guise,
Awaits to soar, the reluctant rise.

Coffee brews, the aroma's grace,
Fleeting hope in every trace.
I take a breath, the moment's here,
To step outside, conquer the fear.

Unfolding warmth, the sun does shine,
I gather strength, the world is mine.
Each stride I take, a choice I find,
The path ahead, I leave behind.

Repose's Rebellion

In the quiet of the night, I dwell,
A calm facade, but tales to tell.
Whispers of dreams rise from the bed,
Rebellion brews beneath my head.

Stars twinkle down, a daring spark,
A restless heart ignites the dark.
Every sigh, a bid for flight,
Against the peace, I seek the night.

Shadows dance, they call my name,
Sleep, they say, yet I feel the flame.
The world outside, a wild tune,
A siren's song beneath the moon.

I'll trade repose for vibrant thrill,
In this rebellion, I find my will.
With every pulse, my spirit's plea,
Embrace the dawn, let it be free.

Songs from Beneath the Covers

Under the sheets, where secrets hide,
A world unfolds, uncurbed and wide.
Soft lullabies of dreams take flight,
In silence whispered through the night.

Each blanket holds a story dear,
Of laughter shared, of laughter near.
The warmth surrounds like a lover's touch,
In these safe confines, we mean so much.

A symphony of thoughts unsung,
Where hopes are born, and fears are flung.
Cocooned in peace, we dare to dream,
In twilight realms, we find our theme.

When morning breaks, will we arise?
Or linger here, 'neath woven skies?
In cozy corners, life's sweet embrace,
We'll weave our songs, in gentle grace.

Rhythm of Regretful Mornings

The clock ticks softly, a mournful sound,
Echoing choices that linger around.
Each moment spent in quiet despair,
A rhythm echoes, I wish to repair.

Sunshine breaks through, yet shadows play,
A haunting melody of yesterday.
With every ray, a memory stings,
The heartache clings to the hope it brings.

Steps feel heavy, like echoes of yore,
I tread with caution, afraid to explore.
Yet in the gloom, a flicker persists,
A promise awaits through the morning mist.

So I embrace this sorrowful beat,
In each regret, a lesson discreet.
Though burdened thoughts may weigh me down,
I'll rise anew, reclaim my crown.

The Cascade of Comfort

In the morning light, soft and sweet,
Warm blankets embrace, a tender retreat.
Whispers of dreams linger still,
Time drips slowly, against my will.

The world outside calls, yet I stay,
Wrapped in the softness, I wish to play.
Each sigh of ease, a gentle song,
In this cascade, I feel I belong.

Coffee waits, but I resist,
In comfort's arms, I can't help but exist.
Moments like these, so precious and rare,
I close my eyes, without a care.

Let the day shimmer without me,
In this pool of comfort, I roam free.
A cascade that flows, warm and bright,
In the heart of my home, it feels so right.

Dawn's Reluctant Chorus

Creaking floorboards break the dawn,
Softly glow the lights, yet I yawn.
Birds sing sweetly outside my pane,
Yet in my mind, it's still a refrain.

The sun peeks in, a shy hello,
But my eyelids weigh, moving slow.
A chorus of brilliance, calling me near,
Yet my dreams hold tight, whispering here.

With pillows piled, a fortress high,
I wonder why I ever comply.
The world awakens, I feel so torn,
In this dance of night, I was reborn.

Yet the call of dawn pulls me through,
With every note, life's promises renew.
I rise, though hesitant, to greet the day,
Dawn's chorus sings, guiding my way.

An Ode to Oversleeping

Oh, sweet surrender to slumber's embrace,
In the arms of the night, I find my place.
Time slips away in a gentle sigh,
Oversleeping feels like flying high.

The world may rush, but I drift in bliss,
A cocoon of warmth, a moment like this.
Sleep's gentle whispers call me to stay,
In the vast expanse where dreams play.

Morning breaks softly, but I stay locked tight,
In the comfort of shadows, avoiding the light.
Freedom found in a canvas of dreams,
I float on clouds, where nothing redeems.

So here's my ode to this peaceful delay,
Where time has no meaning, come what may.
In the tapestry woven by night's gentle hand,
Oversleeping's the magic, so beautifully planned.

Surrender to the Snooze

The morning alarm sings its harsh tune,
Yet my heart yearns for the embrace of the moon.
With heavy eyelids, I plead for more,
To surrender to snooze, oh, I adore.

Five minutes more, I whisper and plead,
A tempting promise, my soul takes heed.
Nestled in comfort, I find my cocoon,
Wrapped in enchantment, morning's monsoon.

The world outside waits, but I linger and dream,
In these extra moments, life feels supreme.
With an echo of laughter, time seems to pause,
In the arms of snooze, I find my cause.

But soon the day beckons, bold and bright,
Yet I linger here, clinging to the night.
In this gentle surrender, I hold my ground,
For in the snooze, pure joy can be found.

Ballad of Bedtime Babble

Whispers of dreams ignite the night,
Softly the stars, they twinkle bright.
Pillows hug heads, shadows take flight,
As lullabies weave through fading light.

Tales of adventures in slumber land,
With creatures and wonders, hand in hand.
Close your eyes, let worries disband,
In the cradle of night, together we stand.

The moon sings a tune, so sweet and low,
Guiding the dreams where soft breezes blow.
Visions of joy in a gentle flow,
In this cozy realm, love's seeds we sow.

Sleepyhead dreams, wrapped in a shawl,
Time drifts like whispers, a soft night call.
With bedtime babble, we softly enthrall,
In the heart of the night, we find our all.

A Drowsy Daydream

Golden rays spill through the window wide,
A tapestry of light where hopes reside.
In drowsy corners, our thoughts collide,
As clouds drift slowly, our worries slide.

Languid moments, slow as the tide,
Wrapped in dreams where visions glide.
A gentle sigh, a peaceful guide,
In the realm of daydreams, we safely bide.

Time floats like feathers, soft and slow,
In lazy hours, we let go.
With every heartbeat, we start to know,
The beauty in stillness begins to grow.

In this world of drift and sway,
Let troubles fade, let worries stray.
A drowsy daydream, come what may,
Is where our spirits find their play.

Harmony of Half-Closed Eyes

In twilight whispers, the world grows dim,
With half-closed eyes, we gently swim.
In pools of silence, our hearts brim,
Each soft breath, a melodic hymn.

Moonlight dances, soft and serene,
A tapestry woven in shades of green.
In this quiet moments, we glean,
The secrets of dreams, a magical scene.

Night draws near with a fragrant sigh,
As stars blanket the vast, dark sky.
With harmony found, we gently lie,
In the arms of slumber, we softly fly.

A lull in the chaos, a pause in the chase,
With half-closed eyes, we embrace grace.
In unity of hearts, we find our place,
In the harmony of night, we learn to face.

Midnight's Last Dance

The clock strikes twelve, a haunting chime,
In shadows deep, we lose all time.
As dreams entwine with stars that climb,
We twirl and spin in night's soft rhyme.

A waltz of whispers fills the air,
Where echoes linger, dreams declare.
With every heartbeat, we shed our care,
In midnight's last dance, we find our flair.

Eclipsing the fears that held us tight,
We sway in the glow of the silvery light.
With laughter and love, we embrace the night,
In the warmth of the dreamscape, everything's right.

As dawn approaches, the stars fade away,
But the memory lingers, a sweet bouquet.
In midnight's last dance, forever we'll stay,
Where shadows retreat, and dreams softly play.

Tapestry of Tiredness

Threads of fatigue weave and intertwine,
A cloak of heaviness, worn like a shrine.
Eyes heavy-lidded, dreams start to blur,
In moments of stillness, whispers confer.

Shadows retreat, as daylight creeps in,
But the yearning for rest feels like a sin.
Wrapped in exhaustion, a silent embrace,
Time drips slowly, in this weary space.

Yet in the stillness, a glimmer of hope,
A break in the fabric, a way to elope.
To drift through the night, where burdens are light,
In the tapestry's folds, find solace and flight.

So thread by thread, we stitch and we mend,
This tapestry woven, our days never end.
In each frayed corner, a memory lies,
A reminder that rest is a gift in disguise.

The Soliloquy of Snoozing

In the quiet chambers of half-closed eyes,
A voice whispers softly, a lullaby sighs.
Time drips like honey, slow and sweet,
As dreams bloom gently, a world to meet.

Shadows of thoughts swirl, dance in the night,
A soliloquy woven with sparkles of light.
Whispers of comfort in the depths of sleep,
Where secrets and wishes are buried so deep.

With each gentle breath, the worries diffuse,
Wrapped in the silence, it's peace we choose.
In the theater of dark, the mind takes its stage,
As we've all learned well, rest turns a page.

So let the snooze gather strength for tomorrow,
In dreams, shed the weight, release all the sorrow.
A soliloquy sung in the echoes of dusk,
Awaits the heart's rhythm, alive and robust.

Muffled Alarms and Silent Battles

Muffled alarms ringing, a call to arise,
Yet the body protests, with heavy-set sighs.
An internal war rages, whispers of dread,
Battles of comfort, where daily dreams tread.

The dawn makes its entrance, light spills like gold,
But the heart seeks the shadows, the stories untold.
A struggle for solace in a world that demands,
Muffled alarms ringing, a war at our hands.

Silent battles waged in the depths of the soul,
Fighting for moments that make us feel whole.
Each yawn is a truce, each stretch a retreat,
In the tug-of-war of an unyielding beat.

Yet if we listen closely, the peace can be found,
In the quiet of stillness, where hope is unbound.
Muffled alarms fade as the heart finds its song,
In the silent battles, we ultimately belong.

Covenant with Comfort

In the embrace of night, a pact softly sworn,
To cradle the weary, where dreams are reborn.
A covenant made with the whispers of rest,
In the arms of comfort, we feel truly blessed.

The pillow, a throne, where thoughts intertwine,
Wrapped in the softness, it feels so divine.
A blanket of warmth, like a tender caress,
Holding all worries, it eases our stress.

In this sacred space, we gently let go,
Of burdens and chaos, of all that we know.
With each slow heartbeat, the night takes its claim,
In a covenant forged, we whisper our name.

So rest in the promise, let dreams drift along,
In the haven of comfort, we find our sweet song.
Together we linger, in silence we trust,
A covenant with comfort, as soft as the dusk.

The Fond Farewell to Morning

The sun peeks over, gentle and bright,
A soft embrace bids the night goodnight.
Birds begin singing, a glorious tune,
Whispers of dawn in the heart of June.

Shadows retreat, the light dances free,
Waking the petals on each blooming tree.
The world stirs awake, a glorious throng,
In this warm moment, we all belong.

With every ray, hopes begin to unfurl,
A fond farewell to the dreams in a swirl.
Morning's sweet laughter, a song in the air,
Carving the silence with beauty so rare.

So let us cherish this spectral display,
In the soft glow of the starting day.
The fond farewell to what once was dark,
Ignites in our spirits a radiant spark.

The Routine of Rest

Moonlight shimmers on clouds drifting slow,
A cozy retreat where dreams freely flow.
Pillows embrace in a tender caress,
In the routine of rest, we find our finesse.

Soft sheets entwine, a cocoon of delight,
Time slips away, but we hold on tight.
The hum of the world fades gently away,
As night wraps around us, a velvety sway.

Each breath a rhythm, a dance of the night,
Guiding us softly till dawn brings the light.
Wrapped in the warmth of slumber's sweet kiss,
In the routine of rest, we find our bliss.

So let the hours drift, unhindered and free,
In dreams, we explore what we wish to see.
With the stars as our guide, together we cling,
In the stillness of night, our souls softly sing.

Chronicles of a Sleepy Morning

A sleepy dawn unfolds in misty grace,
Dreams linger still in this tender space.
Eyes flutter open, gently they blink,
In the chronicles written in shades of think.

The kettle sings sweet, a whispering tune,
Steam curls like magic beneath the soft moon.
Cups cradle warmth in cool morning air,
Each sip a reminder of moments we share.

Soft hues of gold ignite the wide sky,
Clouds drift like secrets, floating on high.
We gather our thoughts, let go of the night,
In the chronicles of morning, everything feels right.

Time bends softly, a noontime embrace,
As laughter and murmurs fill up the space.
In this sleepy morning, we find our way,
Chronicles written till the end of the day.

An Age of Alarms

In the hush of dawn, first whispers arise,
An age of alarms, breaking the skies.
Buzzers and beeps fill the tranquil air,
As dreams turn to echoes, caught unaware.

Blankets are tossed; a sleepy dismay,
The comfort of night instantly gives way.
With a yawn and a stretch, we face the new light,
Navigating through this once-quiet night.

Coffee brews slowly, scents fill the space,
An age of alarms, we pick up the pace.
As feet touch the ground, the world comes alive,
In the hustle and bustle, we learn to survive.

Yet somewhere inside, a stillness remains,
Amidst all the chaos, a beauty that reigns.
For in every alarm, a call to awake,
An age of alarms, where new paths we take.

Milton Keynes UK
Ingram Content Group UK Ltd.
UKHW020734301124
451807UK00019B/785